Gr**e**En

Gina D. B. Clemen

M Great English ONARCHS

and their Times

Den VIII february werde onthalst Maria

Activities by Gina D. B. Clemen and Eleanor Donaldson

Editor: Emma Berridge
Design: Nadia Maestri

We would like to thank:
The Bridgeman Art Library; Kunsthistorisches Museum, Vienna; The National
Portrait Gallery, London; The Royal Collection © 1999, Her Majesty Queen
Elizabeth II;
The Scottish National Portrait Gallery; National Maritime Museum, London;
Woburn Abbey, Bedfordshire; The Royal Archives © 1999, Her Majesty Queen
Elizabeth II.

We would also like to thank Laura Stagno for her contribution to
the 'Reading' a Painting dossiers.

First edition: January 2000

We would be happy to receive your comments and
suggestions, and give you any other information
concerning our material.

www.blackcat-cideb.com

CISQ **CISQ CERT**
**TEXTBOOKS AND
TEACHING MATERIALS**
The quality of the publisher's
design, production and sales processes has
been certified to the standard of
UNI EN ISO 9001

ISBN 978-88-530-0423-9 Book + CD

Printed in Italy by Litoprint, Genoa

CONTENTS

This text is recorded in full.

This symbol indicates the track number
on the accompanying recording.

PART ONE

Henry VIII –
A Tudor King

Portrait of Henry VIII, by Hans Holbein the Younger
(1497(8)-1543). © Belvoir Castle/Bridgeman Art Library.

Introduction

To understand the English monarchs it is important to understand their times. Today some of their actions seem cruel or extravagant. But remember that their times were very different from ours.

A king or queen of the 16th century had unlimited power. Everyone wanted to please the monarch. Rebels or enemies were eliminated. Executions were a common event in Europe.

Henry VIII was the son of Henry VII, the first Tudor King.

He became king during the Renaissance, a time of great change. The Renaissance brought new ideas to art, science and philosophy. However, many of these new ideas clashed [1] with the Catholic Church. So, the church and religion changed with the Reformation. [2] The geography of the world changed too. Explorers discovered new lands, new people and new products.

All his life Henry VIII desperately wanted a male heir [3] to keep the Tudors on the throne of England.

He had a very complex personality. He had his faults but he was a brilliant, talented man and an unforgettable monarch.

1. **clashed** : did not agree.
2. **Reformation** : Protestant reform movement in the Christian Church.
3. **male heir** [eəː] : (here) a son who will become king when his father dies.

THE YOUNG KING

Henry VIII became king in 1509, just before his eighteenth birthday. Young Henry was not prepared to be king. He became king only because his elder brother, Arthur, died at the age of fifteen.

Soon after the coronation Henry married his first wife, Catherine of Aragon, who was his brother Arthur's widow. [1]

Catherine was the only child of King Ferdinand of Spain. Spain was then a very powerful country. This marriage created a strong alliance between the two countries.

Catherine was beautiful and intelligent, and Henry loved her. For almost twenty years they were the perfect royal couple and were happy together.

The new King looked like a hero. Henry was handsome and robust. He was six foot (1.83 metres) tall. At that time most men were about five foot four inches (1.60 metres) tall. He had bright

---

1. **widow** : a woman whose husband is dead.

blue eyes and red hair. He also had a strong personality. The people of England liked King Henry.

Young Henry was strong and full of energy. He loved playing tennis, riding horses and hunting. He hunted in the forests with hawks. [1] He was a very skilled swordsman [2] and loved mock [3] fights called jousts. [4]

Henry was also a great scholar. He spoke English, French, Latin and Spanish. He studied ancient Greek, religious writings, mathematics and astronomy. He was an avid reader [5] and encouraged others to read too. He loved music and played several

Henry VIII jousts before Catherine of Aragon (1511).

1. **hawks** :
2. **skilled swordsman** : this person is good at using a sword.
3. **mock** : imitation.
4. **jousts** : see the picture above.
5. **avid reader** : this person loves reading.

Catherine of Aragon, by Michael Sittow.
Kunsthistorisches Museum, Vienna.

instruments very well: the harp, the organ, the lute [1] and the virginals. [2] He was a good singer and dancer, and also composed beautiful songs. We can still listen to some of his compositions.

During this time the Renaissance developed in England. King Henry was a patron of the arts. Writers, poets, painters and musicians were all welcome at his court. The famous Dutch scholar, Erasmus, was Henry's friend.

The young King was very busy with banquets, dancing, hunting and sports. He decorated his castles and palaces with beautiful furniture and paintings. He wore expensive clothes and jewellery, and was generous with his friends.

Henry did not have much time to govern his country. One of his advisers [3] began to govern England. His name was Thomas Wolsey, a clever man of humble [4] origins. He was a cardinal of the Church.

Henry desperately wanted an heir to the Tudor throne. Early in 1511 Catherine gave birth to a son. There were great celebrations, but the little Prince died after two months. King Henry was very disappointed.

1. **lute** :
2. **virginals** : piano-like musical instruments of the 16-17th centuries.
3. **advisers** : these people give their opinion and help make decisions.
4. **humble** : of a low social class, poor.

UNDERSTANDING THE TEXT

⚠ COMPREHENSION

Go back to the text. For each question, put a tick (✔) in the box next to the correct answer.

1. Henry VIII became king in 1509
   - a. ☐ just after his fifteenth birthday.
   - b. ☐ just before his eighteenth birthday.
   - c. ☐ when his sister died.

2. Henry's first wife, Catherine of Aragon, was
   - a. ☐ King Ferdinand's sister.
   - b. ☐ his brother's best friend.
   - c. ☐ his brother's widow.

3. Young Henry was tall and strong,
   - a. ☐ but he was not very handsome.
   - b. ☐ but he hated fighting.
   - c. ☐ and he loved hunting and sports.

4. He was a great scholar and
   - a. ☐ an excellent musician.
   - b. ☐ a good painter.
   - c. ☐ a courageous explorer.

5. During Henry's reign
   - a. ☐ there were wars between England and Spain.
   - b. ☐ the Middle Ages began.
   - c. ☐ the Renaissance took place in England.

6. Thomas Wolsey began to govern the country
   - a. ☐ when Henry's brother died.
   - b. ☐ because young Henry was busy with banquets, hunting and sports.
   - c. ☐ because young Henry became very ill.

7. King Henry was very unhappy when
   - a. ☐ his two-month old son died.
   - b. ☐ Cardinal Wolsey began to govern the country.
   - c. ☐ Catherine of Aragon died.

THE PAST SIMPLE

Go back to Chapter One and underline in pencil the Past Simple of the following verbs. Then write the Past Simple and the Past Participle of each verb in the correct column.

Infinitive	Past Simple	Past Participle
to become		
to be		
to die		
to marry		
to love		
to look		
to have		
to speak		
to study		
to play		
to develop		
to wear		
to begin		
to want		

Now circle the regular verbs in the first column in green and the irregular verbs in red.

LANGUAGE

He loved playing tennis, riding horses and hunting...
He played several instruments very well.

> **Like**, **love** and **hate** are usually followed by a verb + -ing:
> * *I love travelling but I hate flying.*
>
> To describe our abilities we can say we **are good at something** or that
> we **can do something well**.
> **Can** or **could** are always followed by the infinitive without 'to':
> * *He is good at running and he can play basketball very well.*

a. Make a list of things Henry VIII liked doing, or could do well.

b. What are the people doing in the pictures?
   Do you like any of these activities? Can you do any of them?

1

2

3

4

c. Make a list of other activities you like or are good at.

4 **Put the letters in order to make eight different types of music.**

a. cislaclsa ....

b. lesub ....

c. opp ....

d. uehso ....

e. eegarg ....

f. adhr kocr ....

g. kunp ....

h. lokf ....

5 **LISTENING**

Go back to track 3. Listen to the music again. It was written by Henry VIII.

a. When you listen to this music, can you imagine people dancing at Henry's court?

b. Do you recognise any of the musical instruments?

c. Does it sound like any rock group you know?

d. Could you dance to this type of music?

e. Can you play a musical instrument?

T: GRADE 5

6 **Topic – Music**

Now ask and answer these questions.

a. What type(s) of music do you like to listen to?

b. Who is your favourite group, singer or composer?

c. Have you ever been to a pop concert or music festival? Which singer(s)/group(s) did you see?

PROJECT **ON THE WEB**

Your teacher will give you the correct web-site address. Find out more about the Renaissance in Europe. Answer these questions, then discuss your answers with another student.

a. 'Renaissance' is a French word. What does it mean in English?

b. In which period did the Renaissance take place?

c. The Renaissance was a time of change and new ideas, when compared with Medieval times or 'The Middle Ages'. In which areas of life were the biggest changes seen?

d. Can you name at least two famous people from this time? What did they do?

CHAPTER TWO

WAR, PEACE AND TAXES

King Henry was a very ambitious man. He wanted the glory of a war and in 1512 he invaded France, unsuccessfully.

The following year Henry was more successful. The English won a battle that Henry called 'The Battle of the Spurs'.

While Henry was in France, the Scottish King, James IV, invaded northern England. After a violent battle the English won at Flodden Field. King James IV and thousands of Scots were killed.

Henry was pleased with the success in France and he wanted to return the following year. However, the war cost a lot of money and only a little land was conquered.

Henry's adviser, Cardinal Thomas Wolsey, did not want another war. He convinced Henry to make peace with France.

He was a very ambitious and greedy man. [1] In 1515 he became Lord Chancellor [2] of England. He was the most powerful man in the country after the King. Wolsey became very rich. He used his money to build the 1,000-room palace of Hampton Court. He later gave it to Henry to win his favour.

During this period there were many religious problems. The Catholic Church was very powerful and very rich. Many people in England did not like the Church or the priests. They were tired of paying high taxes to the Church.

In October 1517 a German monk [3] called Martin Luther protested against the Catholic Church. He wanted to make radical changes. This was the beginning of the Reformation and the Protestant Church.

Henry did not like Martin Luther's ideas and wrote the 'Defence of the Seven Sacraments.' He dedicated it to Pope Leo X. The Pope was pleased and gave Henry the title of 'Defender of the Faith.'

For eight years Cardinal Wolsey kept peace with France. In 1520 he organised a meeting in Picardy in France between the two Kings. Wolsey wanted the Kings to sign a peace treaty.

Elaborate tents made of gold cloth and a beautiful palace were created for the two Kings and their courts. The entire English court of 5,800 people went to Picardy. There were jousts and elaborate banquets. An immense amount of money was spent for

1. **greedy man** : this man wants to have more of something, (here) power and money.

2. **Lord Chancellor** : a very important person (in the English government).

3. **monk** : a member of a group of religious men.

CARDINAL WOOLSEY

Thomas Wolsey, by an unknown artist.
By courtesy of The National Portrait Gallery, London.

this occasion. Henry wore a cloak [1] made of gold cloth. The extravagant finery [2] gave the place of the meeting its name, 'The

1. **cloak** : a long coat.
2. **finery** : beautiful clothes and ornaments.

Field of the Cloth of Gold.' The two Kings signed a peace treaty, but after two years they were at war again.

The Field of the Cloth of Gold, by an unknown artist.
The Royal Collection © 1999, Her Majesty Queen Elizabeth II.

Henry and his court lived in luxury. His clothes and jewels became more and more magnificent. Henry soon spent most of his father's money.

During almost 20 years of marriage Catherine gave birth to four sons, but they all died. Only a girl, Princess Mary, survived. [1] Henry was desperate. He didn't want a daughter. He wanted a son to become king after his death. Catherine was too old to have other children and Henry lost interest in her.

---

1. **survived** : continued to live.

UNDERSTANDING THE TEXT

 SUMMARY

Fill in the gaps with the words below.

taxes   luxury   Catholic Church
peace   Catherine
meeting   Lord Chancellor
ambitious   Picardy
money   son   Reformation
killed   France (x2)
religion   English

a. In 1513 Henry went to war against ....

b. King James IV and thousands of Scots were .... at Flodden Field after a battle with the ....

c. Cardinal Wolsey was very .... and became .... of England in 1515.

d. The early sixteenth century was a period of radical change for the Christian .... in Western Europe.

e. During this period the Catholic Church was very rich and powerful. Many people were tired of paying high .... to the Church.

f. The .... began with Martin Luther's protest against the ....

g. Henry and his court went to .... to sign a .... treaty with the King of .... The place of the .... was called 'The Field of the Cloth of Gold.'

h. Henry soon spent most of his father's .... because he and his court lived in ....

i. .... did not give Henry a .... so he lost interest in her.

21

You are King Henry VIII. You send this letter to your friend, the great scholar Erasmus, in Rotterdam, telling him all about your meeting with the King of France at the 'Field of the Cloth of Gold'.
Re-write the letter. Put the verbs in the Past Simple tense, and add the missing words to make full, correct sentences.

Dear Erasmus,

Lord Chancellor Wolsey / organise / important meeting / Picardy / between myself / King of France.
My court / I / leave England / Wednesday.
We / have / good sea voyage.
When / we arrive / it / be / sunny day.
I / wear / my precious cloak.
Everyone / be / amazed.
I / bring / a lot of / splendid clothes / jewels.
On Friday / I / go hunting / in / forest.
On Saturday / there be / a joust.
I / win / of course!
It / be / great fun.
On Sunday / the King / invite / my court / to / magnificent banquet.
We / eat / for seven hours!
Then / we / go / to sleep.

Your friend,
Henry

'Reading' a Painting

In the past artists often painted or sculpted portraits of important people. Before photography was invented there was no other way to represent them. These portraits showed what people were like and how they lived. Portraits were not always true representations of the person. Some people wanted to appear young or good-looking when in reality they were not. When a painting is a true representation of the person, we say the portrait is 'realistic'. When the painting looks better than the person, we say that the portrait is 'idealised'.

Look at the portrait of Henry VIII on page 25.

Look at his clothes. They are made of velvet, silk and fur. There is a lot of gold on his cloak and he is wearing rings on both hands. During Henry's time men wore gold rings with precious stones.

Clothes were very expensive and it often took many years to make them. Several people worked on one piece of clothing. The best clothes could cost as much as whole ships. The children of the nobility wore elaborate clothes like adults. The poor wore very simple clothes.

Look at his legs. He has a ribbon called a garter on his left leg. It has the motto of the Order of the Garter, the highest order of Knighthood, written in old French.

Look at how big Henry's body is. When he was older, he became so fat that he was taken to his many palaces in a special vehicle on wheels because he could not walk far.

Henry is standing on a splendid Persian carpet. Notice the elaborate tapestry behind him.

LOOKING AT THE PAINTING
Look at the painting and answer these questions.

a. What are the main colours in this painting?

b. Look at the background. Apart from the tapestry and the Persian carpet, the background is very simple. In your opinion, this is because

☐ the King did not have any furniture in this room.

☐ the painter was not able to paint any other type of background.

☐ the painter wanted to concentrate all his attention on the King.

c. It was common to have tapestries like the one in the painting on the walls of big houses or castles. Why do you think this was?

☐ to make the rooms darker

☐ to show how rich the owner was

☐ to make the rooms warmer

d. Choose words from the box to describe King Henry VIII in this portrait.

> arrogant   beautiful   large   powerful   happy
> surprised   strong   round   fat   slim   angry   severe

In your opinion, which words best describe his face and his appearance?

Example: *He's got a beautiful face, he looks powerful.*

 For ordinary people clothes were very expensive. But the king had beautiful clothes and expensive jewellery. Think about clothes in your country today and answer these questions.

a. What type of clothes do rich people buy today?

b. Why do you think clothes are cheaper to make today than they were in Henry VIII's time?

c. Do you buy a lot of clothes? What sort of clothes do you buy?

d. What colours are fashionable this year?

Portrait of Henry VIII, by Hans Holbein the Younger (1497(8)-1543).
© Belvoir Castle/Bridgeman Art Library.

CHAPTER THREE

THE BREAK
WITH ROME

Early in 1526 Henry met a young English lady of the court. Her name was Anne Boleyn. She had long, black hair and dark eyes. She spoke French and wore elegant French clothes. She was very lively, intelligent and interested in politics. Henry fell in love with her immediately. Several men of the court fell in love with her too. Anne had a sixth finger on her left hand. Her enemies called her a witch. [1]

Henry wanted to marry Anne Boleyn and have a son with her. He decided to divorce Catherine, but he needed permission from the Pope in Rome. He asked Cardinal Wolsey to convince the Pope. After a few years the Pope refused the divorce.

Henry was furious with Wolsey and the Church. He accused Cardinal Wolsey of treason [2] and he died soon after. In 1529 Henry

1. **witch** : this woman has magical powers.

2. **treason** : disloyalty to one's monarch and/or country.

Anne Boleyn, by an unknown artist.
By courtesy of The National Portrait Gallery, London.

chose Sir Thomas More, a great scholar and an honest man, as Lord Chancellor of England. Sir Thomas More was Lord Chancellor until 1532 when he was beheaded [1] because he opposed Henry's break with Rome.

In 1533 Henry also chose a new Archbishop of Canterbury, Thomas Cranmer. Cranmer wanted to change the Church. He believed in the absolute power of the King. Cranmer encouraged the use of the Bible in English. He also helped to establish the Protestant Church in England. He later annulled Henry's marriage to Catherine of Aragon.

In January 1533 Henry and Anne Boleyn were secretly married. Catherine of Aragon was banished [2] from court and died alone three years later.

By May 1533 Anne Boleyn was Queen of England. Four months later she gave birth to Princess Elizabeth. Another girl! Henry was desolate. He wanted a son more than anything.

In 1534 Thomas Cromwell, Henry's new Lord Chancellor, helped put into effect the Act of Supremacy. With this Act Henry became the Supreme Head of the Church of England.

Henry was soon tired of Anne because she did not give him a son. He then met another lady called Jane Seymour and fell in love with her.

Anne, Henry's second wife, was accused of adultery and treason. She was imprisoned in the Tower of London and was beheaded in May 1536.

Eleven days after Anne Boleyn's execution Henry married Jane Seymour. She was a quiet, docile lady who brought happiness to

---

1. **beheaded** : his head was cut off.
2. **banished** : sent away.

Jane Seymour, by Hans Holbein the Younger (1497(8)-1543).
Kunsthistorisches Museum, Vienna.

the royal family.

In October 1537 Jane gave birth to a son, Prince Edward. King Henry was overjoyed [1] and the whole country celebrated. Unfortunately, after twelve days the Queen died from an infection.

Henry mourned [2] her for a long time. Jane, his third wife, was probably his favourite.

Henry now had an heir – Prince Edward was the future King of England. He was first in succession to the throne because he was a male. Edward was intelligent and received an excellent education from the best scholars.

To show his power and importance Henry VIII built magnificent palaces such as St James' Palace and Whitehall Palace. He also built castles and more than fifty houses around England.

1. **overjoyed** : very happy.
2. **mourned** : cried and was very sad after her death.

UNDERSTANDING THE TEXT

COMPREHENSION

**Decide if each sentence is correct or incorrect. If it is correct, mark A.
If it is not correct, mark B.**

      A   B

1 Anne Boleyn came from France and she
could not speak any English. ☐ ☐

2 Henry fell in love with Anne Boleyn, but he needed
permission from Cardinal Wolsey to divorce
his wife. ☐ ☐

3 Henry was furious with Cardinal Wolsey and
the Church when the Pope refused the divorce. ☐ ☐

4 Thomas Cranmer became the new Lord
Chancellor of England, and Sir Thomas More
became the new Archbishop of Canterbury. ☐ ☐

5 The new Archbishop of Canterbury permitted Henry
to divorce from Catherine and marry Anne Boleyn. ☐ ☐

6 Princess Elizabeth was born in 1533, and Henry was
very happy. ☐ ☐

7 In 1534 Henry became the Supreme Head of the
English Church. ☐ ☐

8 In May 1536 Anne Boleyn was banished and Henry
married Jane Seymour. ☐ ☐

9 Jane Seymour gave birth to Prince Edward but died
soon after. ☐ ☐

10 Prince Edward received an excellent education
from his father. ☐ ☐

11 Henry VIII only had one home, St James' Palace. ☐ ☐

Now rewrite the incorrect sentences with the correct information.

2 Choose the words from the 'Tudor rose' (see page 35) to describe these people. Some words can be used more than once. Then choose two people and write a few sentences about them. Use your notebook if you don't have enough space.

patron of the arts
rich   great scholar
wore magnificent clothes   greedy
honest man   ambitious
opposed Henry's break with Rome
Lord Chancellor   was beheaded
organised a meeting in France
built palaces and castles
built Hampton Court
lived in luxury

Wolsey   More   Henry VIII

....

....

....

....

....

3 'All about Anne'
Are the following sentences right (R) or wrong (W)? If there isn't enough information to answer 'Right' or 'Wrong' choose 'Doesn't say' (DS).

a. Anne Boleyn was a young English lady of the court.
   R ☐   W ☐   DS ☐

b. She was twenty-two years old.
   R ☐   W ☐   DS ☐

c. She spoke Spanish very well.
   R ☐   W ☐   DS ☐

d. Henry wanted to marry Anne and have a son with her.
   R ☐   W ☐   DS ☐

e. She had six fingers on both hands.
   R ☐   W ☐   DS ☐

f. She was imprisoned in the Tower of London and was beheaded.
   R ☐   W ☐   DS ☐

g. Anne's father was a famous scholar.
   R ☐   W ☐   DS ☐

4 **SPEAKING**
Class discussion – witchcraft and superstition

a. Find the words 'witchcraft' and 'superstition' in a dictionary. What do they mean?

b. People said Anne Boleyn was a witch because she had six fingers on her left hand. At that time people did not have scientific explanations for natural events. They believed certain objects or actions could bring bad luck.
   Look at these superstitions about good or bad luck. Do they exist in your country? What other things can bring good or bad luck?
   1. If you are worried about something, cross your fingers or touch wood to help bring good luck.
   2. If a black cat crosses your path, be careful, a witch could make trouble for you.
   3. Spilling salt can bring bad luck. To protect yourself from it, throw salt over your left shoulder with your right hand.

CHAPTER FOUR

HENRY'S LATER YEARS

n Henry's time there were about 850 monasteries in England
and Wales. The religious orders obeyed the Pope in Rome
and not King Henry.

The monasteries had rich treasures and a quarter of
all the land in England. Henry needed money so he and
his Lord Chancellor, Cromwell, decided to close the monasteries
and take their treasures and land.

Between 1536 and 1539 Cromwell sent his men to inspect
them. When they returned they said, 'There is corruption in the
monasteries.' This was a good reason to close them.

Cromwell's men took the rich treasures and gave them to the King.
They sent away the monks and nuns. [1] Some monasteries were
destroyed and others were sold to the nobility. Many were
transformed into beautiful houses. The land of the monasteries now
belonged to King Henry, who became the richest monarch in Europe.

1. **nuns** : members of a group of religions women.

Henry's Later Years

With the money from the monasteries Henry built castles and fortifications to protect the south coast of England. Deal Castle

Deal Castle.

in Kent was the biggest fort on the coast. It was built in the form of a rose, the Tudor symbol. Henry also built bigger warships. England now had the most powerful navy in Europe. (Henry's great warship the *Mary Rose* sank [1] in 1545. In 1982 the remains of the ship were found, and now the *Mary Rose* can be seen at the Naval Dockyard in Portsmouth.)

Henry was now forty-eight. He was very fat and his health was not good. He became short-tempered [2] and oppressive. Everyone had to obey him.

The Tudor court still attracted many artists and musicians. Hans Holbein the Younger was a great German artist. He was the King's royal painter. He painted

Tudor rose.

many splendid pictures of the royal family and the Tudor court.

During the 1540s Henry built an extravagant new palace called Nonsuch Palace, in Surrey. A village was destroyed to build it, but it was never completed.

---

1. **sank** : went under water.
2. **short-tempered** : quick to get angry.

Henry's political position in Europe became weak. Spain and France wanted to destroy him. He needed a strong ally. [1] Cromwell convinced Henry to marry a German princess called Anne of Cleves. Henry sent Holbein to Germany to paint her portrait. Holbein painted a lovely portrait of Anne, which convinced Henry to marry her.

When she arrived in England Henry was horribly surprised. She was ugly and fat and some people said she looked like a horse. She didn't speak English or like music. He was very angry with Cromwell, who was accused of treason and beheaded in 1540. Henry married Anne for political reasons and divorced her seven months later in July.

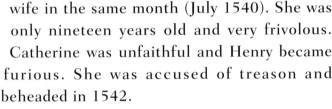

Catherine Howard became Henry's fifth wife in the same month (July 1540). She was only nineteen years old and very frivolous. Catherine was unfaithful and Henry became furious. She was accused of treason and beheaded in 1542.

A gold coin from Tudor times.

At this point of his life Henry wanted a sincere companion and a nurse. He married his last wife, Catherine Parr, in 1543. She was a mature woman of thirty-one, who was gentle and well educated. (In Henry's time most people did not live past forty-five.)

Catherine brought Henry's three children to court and took interest in their education. She was a kind and loving step-mother. [2] She also encouraged Henry to found Trinity College, a part of Oxford university. Henry's last marriage was successful.

1. **ally** : this country is a political friend of another country.
2. **step-mother** : this woman marries one's father after his first wife.

KATHARINE PARRE

Catherine Parr, by an unknown artist.
By courtesy of The National Portrait Gallery, London.

During his later years there were wars with Scotland and France. These wars cost Henry an enormous amount of money. At last he made peace with France in 1546.

Henry's final years were tormented by illness. He was obese. He could not walk and was carried everywhere by servants. He had painful ulcers on his legs, severe headaches and several other illnesses. Catherine Parr nursed [1] him patiently.

In his will [2] he named his three children heirs to the throne.

Henry remained a Catholic all his life. He died on 28 January 1547, and was buried at Windsor next to his third wife, Jane Seymour – the wife he loved the most.

1. **nursed** : took care of.
2. **will** : testament; a person's last written wishes.

UNDERSTANDING THE TEXT

 COMPREHENSION
Circle the correct word.

a. There were approximately 850 *monks / monasteries* in England and *Wales / Scotland* in Henry's time.

b. Henry and *Cromwell / Cranmer* closed the monasteries and took their treasures and land.

c. Henry built *castles / churches* to protect the south coast of England. Deal Castle was built in the form of a *circle / rose*.

d. Hans Holbein the *Elder / Younger* was the King's royal *musician / painter*.

e. Henry married the *German / French* Princess Anne of Cleves because he needed a *rich wife / strong ally*.

f. Henry's *fourth / fifth* queen was *Catherine Howard / Catherine Parr*. She was beheaded because she *had lovers / was fat and ugly*.

g. Henry's last *wife / nurse* was Catherine *Parr / Howard*.

h. In his later years Henry founded Trinity *Castle / College*.

i. During his final years Henry had several *illnesses / wives*. He could not *speak / walk* because he was obese.

j. Before his *marriage / death* in 1547 he named *his son Edward / his three children* heir(s) to the throne.

 Match the name with the place.

NAME		PLACE	
a. ☐	Hans Holbein the Younger	1.	Germany
b. ☐	Pope	2.	Portsmouth
c. ☐	Deal Castle	3.	Surrey
d. ☐	'Mary Rose'	4.	Germany
e. ☐	Nonsuch Palace	5.	Kent
f. ☐	Anne of Cleves	6.	Rome

Listen to the information on the recording more than once if necessary. Then fill in the family tree with the names and the birth dates.

Elizabeth	Charles	Anne	John
Catherine	Edward	Mary	Samuel
James	Jane	William Hodgkins	

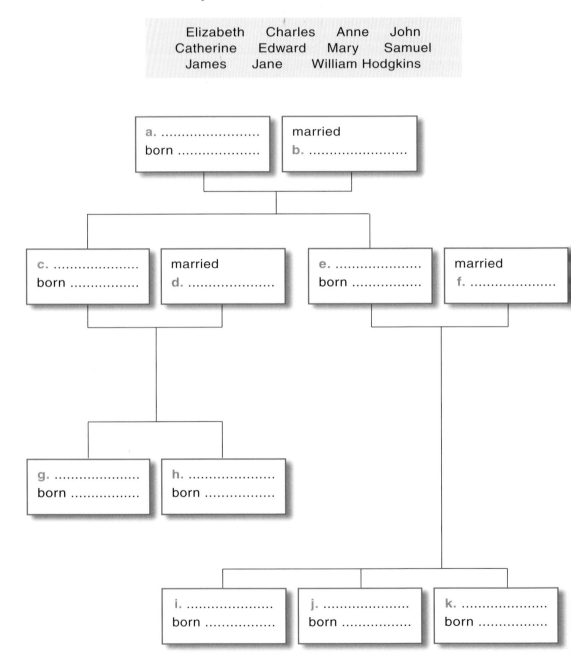

a. ....
born ....

married
b. ....

c. ....
born ....

married
d. ....

e. ....
born ....

married
f. ....

g. ....
born ....

h. ....
born ....

i. ....
born ....

j. ....
born ....

k. ....
born ....

WHO ARE THEY?

Read the description of Henry's six wives and decide who they are.

a. I'm nineteen years old and very pretty. Henry thinks I'm frivolous. But he doesn't understand me. He's too old! I love another man – a young, handsome one. My name is:

☐ Anne of Cleves

☐ Catherine Howard

☐ Anne Boleyn

b. I've got black hair and dark eyes. I speak French and I'm very lively and intelligent. Henry wants to divorce his old wife and marry me! I want to give him a son. I'm:

☐ Anne Boleyn

☐ Jane Seymour

☐ Catherine Parr

c. I'm the step-mother of his three children. Henry is often short-tempered, but I'm very patient. I nurse him and look after his children. My name is:

☐ Catherine of Aragon

☐ Catherine Howard

☐ Catherine Parr

d. Henry and I were happy together for many years. We have a lovely daughter. Now Henry doesn't love me anymore. He wants to divorce me and marry a woman who is a witch! What can I do? I'm:

☐ Jane Seymour

☐ Catherine of Aragon

☐ Anne of Cleves

e. I'm not beautiful, I'm fat, but I am a princess. I don't speak English and I don't like music. My name is:

☐ Jane Seymour

☐ Catherine Parr

☐ Anne of Cleves

f. When Henry met me he fell in love with me. We got married in 1536. I get along well with dear Henry because I'm a quiet, docile person. Soon I will give him a son. I'm his favourite wife. I'm:

☐ Jane Seymour

☐ Anne Boleyn

☐ Catherine Howard

KING HENRY'S WIVES
Complete the table below.
In the first column fill in the missing names of Henry's wives. The dates show when they were married to Henry.
In the second column write *girl, boy* or *no children*.
In the third column write *divorced, died* or *beheaded.*

Name of queen	Children	What happened to her
Catherine of Aragon (1509-1533)	four boys, one girl	divorced
.... Boleyn (1533-1536)		
Jane .... (1536-1537)		
Anne .... (1540-1540)		
Catherine .... (1540-1542)		
.... Parr (1543-1547)		she survived Henry

 WRITING
People think that Henry VIII had a special 'black book' to record information about corruption in the monasteries. If you were in the King's 'black book', the King was not pleased with you because of something you did. Today we say you are 'in someone's black books' if they are not happy about something you did.

a. You are Henry VIII. Make a list of things and people that make you angry.
   Example: I received a letter from the Pope today. He says I cannot marry Anne Boleyn.

b. Now make your own 'black book' of things that make you angry or that you do not like.

PART **TWO**

Elizabeth I –
the Virgin Queen

Elizabeth I when Princess, by an unknown artist.
The Royal Collection © 1999, Her Majesty Queen Elizabeth II.

Introduction

Queen Elizabeth's reign was so important in history that it was called the Elizabethan Age.

During her reign England's progress in the field of discovery and colonisation was immense. Englishmen explored the New World and brought back an incredible amount of riches. Trade began with other countries which helped to develop English commerce.

This was the beginning of English colonisation in the New World.

The Elizabethan Age was also rich in learning. It was the age of Shakespeare, Bacon, Marlowe and other famous names.

Queen Elizabeth I was an exceptional Queen. Like her father, Henry VIII, she was very intelligent and had a strong character. Unlike him, she was just and moderate. Her people loved her greatly. She brought peace, unity and power to her country.

CHAPTER ONE

YOUNG ELIZABETH

Elizabeth was born on 7 September 1533. Her childhood was not happy. She was two years old when her mother, Anne Boleyn, was beheaded. She spent most of her early life at Hatfield House, away from her father, King Henry VIII.

However, Henry wanted his daughter to have the best education. Roger Ascham, a great scholar and humanist, was Elizabeth's private teacher. She was very intelligent, witty [1] and enjoyed learning. She could read, write and speak Latin, Greek, French, Spanish, Italian and Welsh fluently.

Elizabeth loved riding horses, hunting and dancing. Like her father, she had a talent for music and played the lute and the virginals. Unlike her father, she was very thrifty [2] and did not like spending money.

1. **witty** : had an amusing way of speaking.
2. **thrifty** : economical; careful with money.

Elizabeth wasn't beautiful but she was elegant. She was thin, of medium height and very vain. [1] She had red hair, expressive eyes and lovely hands.

When Henry VIII died in 1547, Edward VI became King at the age of nine. But his reign was short. He died of tuberculosis when he was only fifteen.

In 1553 his half-sister, Mary (Catherine of Aragon's daughter), became Queen. Her mother was a Catholic and she wanted England to be a Catholic country again. Protestants were persecuted and almost 300 were killed. For this reason she was also known as 'Bloody Mary'.

Young Elizabeth was in danger because she was a Protestant and was very popular with the people. Queen Mary thought Elizabeth plotted [2] against her and imprisoned her in the Tower of London in 1554. Elizabeth never forgot this terrible experience. After two months Mary freed her.

On the night of 17 November 1558 Queen Mary died. The bells of London rang and everyone celebrated: young Elizabeth was the new Queen.

Elizabeth became queen at the age of 25. Like others of her time, Elizabeth believed in astrology. Her astrologer was John Dee, a famous astronomer. He chose the best day for her coronation ceremony: 15 January 1559.

Elizabeth was loved by the people but she was still in danger. The Kings of France and Spain wanted to invade England and bring back the Catholic faith.

The young Queen was alert, clever and prudent. She carefully

1. **vain** : full of self-admiration.
2. **plotted** : secretly planned to do something wrong.

Robert Dudley, Earl of Leicester, by an unknown artist.
By courtesy of The National Portrait Gallery, London.

chose advisers who were honest, loyal and experienced.

William Cecil was Elizabeth's Secretary of State and her most important minister. He was her dear friend and she trusted him completely. Cecil served her for 40 years. Elizabeth was very wise to choose Matthew Parker as Archbishop of Canterbury. He established a moderate Church of England and created a compromise between Catholics and extreme Protestants.

She also chose Lord Robert Dudley to be part of her court. He was her childhood friend and sweetheart, [1] and remained one of her favourites for many years.

Elizabeth was a strong ruler. England was now a Protestant country. The Act of Supremacy made her Head of the Church of England. All priests had to use the Book of Common Prayer.

The Queen liked meeting her people and was always kind to the old and the sick. She and her court frequently went on tours, or 'progresses', [2] around the country to visit noble subjects. It was an honour to be part of a royal tour. However, the cost of entertaining [3] the Queen and her court was astronomical and several nobles went bankrupt. [4]

1. **sweetheart** : lover.
2. **progresses** : the word used by Elizabeth for her tours.
3. **entertaining** : amusing; giving food, drink and accommodation.
4. **went bankrupt** : (here) became poor.

UNDERSTANDING THE TEXT

 COMPREHENSION

Fill in the gaps with the words below.

advisers   William Cecil   intelligent

tours   Elizabeth   imprisoned

loved   dancing   daughter

favourites   Tower

Protestants   alert

a. Young Elizabeth was very .... and enjoyed riding, hunting and ....

b. Catherine of Aragon's .... , Mary, became Queen and persecuted the ....

c. Queen Mary .... Elizabeth in the .... of London.

d. When Queen Mary died in 1558 .... became Queen of England; she was .... by the people.

e. Elizabeth was .... and clever, and chose her .... carefully.

f. .... was Elizabeth's most important minister. Lord Robert Dudley was one of her ....

g. The Queen liked meeting her people and often went on .... around the country.

VOCABULARY
Find the hidden word
Read the definitions and write the word.

a. very clever ＿ ＿ | ＿ | ＿ ＿ ＿ ＿ ＿ ＿ ＿ ＿

b. Roger Ascham was a ... ＿ ＿ | ＿ | ＿ ＿ ＿ ＿

c. musical instrument ＿ ＿ | ＿ | ＿ ＿ ＿ ＿ ＿ ＿

d. full of self-admiration ＿ ＿ | ＿ | ＿

e. religion ＿ | ＿ ＿ ＿ ＿

f. house where Elizabeth lived ＿ ＿ | ＿ | ＿ ＿ ＿ ＿ ＿

g. can be trusted ＿ ＿ | ＿ | ＿ ＿ ＿

Complete the following sentence with the word in the red column.

Queen Elizabeth was ＿ ＿ ＿ ＿ ＿ ＿ ＿ .

Check the meaning of this word in a dictionary. Find a word or words that mean the opposite.

3 **QUESTION WORDS**
Read the answers then write the questions using *why*, *who*, *when*, *what* and *where* (x2).

a. .... was Elizabeth's mother?
Anne Boleyn.

b. .... did Elizabeth live as a child?
Hatfield House.

c. .... did Queen Mary die?
She died in November 1558.

d. .... colour was Elizabeth's hair?
Her hair was red.

e. .... was young Elizabeth in danger?
Young Elizabeth was in danger because she was a Protestant.

f. .... was she imprisoned?
She was imprisoned in the Tower of London.

SPEAKING

Class discussion

a. Queen Mary and Queen Elizabeth were heads of state.
   - How many other women do you know who were or are now heads of state?
   - Do you think they were/are good rulers? Why? Why not?

b. Astrology is the study of how the sun, moon, stars and planets presumably influence people's lives. Elizabeth believed in astrology, and had her own personal astrologer, John Dee.
   - Do you know your star sign? Find the name of your star sign in English. Is it similar or different in your language?
   - Do you read horoscopes? Do you believe what your horoscope says?
   - Do you think astrology is a science?

 Aries
March 21 – April 20

 Libra
September 23 – October 22

 Taurus
April 21 – May 20

 Scorpio
October 23 – November 21

 Gemini
May 21 – June 20

 Sagittarius
November 22 – December 21

 Cancer
June 21 – July 22

 Capricorn
December 22 – January 20

 Leo
July 23 – August 22

 Aquarius
January 21 – February 19

 Virgo
August 23 – September 22

 Pisces
February 20 – March 20

CHAPTER TWO

PLOTS AND PROBLEMS

ary Stuart was Elizabeth's cousin and her most dangerous rival. She was a Catholic, and many Catholics wanted Mary to be the Queen of England.

Mary was born in Scotland. She was the daughter of James V, King of Scotland, and Mary Guise, a French noblewoman. Mary became Queen when she was only one week old. Since there were political problems in Scotland, Mary went to France at the age of five. She had a happy childhood in the luxurious French court. She married the French Dauphin [1] Francis and became Queen of France for a short time. In 1560 her husband, the young King of France, died and she returned to Scotland.

Scotland was a Protestant country but the Scots accepted her as their Queen. Mary was very beautiful, charming and fun-loving. [2] This worried Queen Elizabeth.

---

1. **Dauphin** : between 1350-1830, the title of the oldest son of the French monarch.
2. **fun-loving** : this person enjoys laughing and having fun.

Plots and Problems

At this time something terrible happened: Elizabeth caught smallpox,[1] a disease that killed many people in those days. She was dangerously ill for many days. Elizabeth's German doctor saved her life. Smallpox scars[2] remained on Elizabeth's face all her life. She always wore white powder and cosmetics to hide the scars.

Parliament wanted Elizabeth to marry as soon as possible. It was important to have an heir to the Tudor throne.

Several foreign monarchs wanted to marry Elizabeth: The Archduke of Austria, Ivan 'the Terrible', Tsar of Russia, the King of France and the King of Spain.

Many noblemen of her court wanted to marry her, too. Sir Christopher Hatton loved her so much that he never married. However, Elizabeth spent most of her time with Robert Dudley, her favourite companion.

Mary Queen of Scots, by an unknown artist. The Scottish National Portrait Gallery.

1. **smallpox** : an infectious disease. It leaves marks on the skin.
2. **scars** : marks on the skin.

Elizabeth was not interested in marriage. She feared that a foreign king was dangerous for England. And she did not want to share her power with anyone.

In 1566, Robert Dudley, the Earl of Leicester, said, 'I really believe the Queen will never marry.' He was right. However, Parliament insisted. One day Elizabeth became angry and said,

Execution of Mary Queen of Scots, by an unknown artist.
The Scottish National Portrait Gallery.

Plots and Problems

'I am already bound unto [1] a husband, which is the kingdom of England!'

Elizabeth was afraid of a bad marriage. She had the example of her mother and of her cousin, Mary Stuart. After returning to Scotland, Mary married her cousin, Lord Darnley, in 1565. Soon after the marriage she hated him. Early in 1567 Darnley was killed. Many people suspected Mary and her lover, the Earl of Bothwell. When she married the Earl of Bothwell the Scots were furious and she escaped to England.

Mary was now a real danger for the Queen – she was on English soil. [2] Catholic nobles began plotting against Elizabeth in favour of Mary. Elizabeth decided to imprison Mary in a remote castle. She remained there for 19 years. Other plots against Elizabeth were discovered, but she didn't want to execute her cousin. In 1586 Mary was finally accused of treason, and in 1587 she was beheaded.

1. **bound unto** : (archaic) married to.
2. **soil** : land, ground.

UNDERSTANDING THE TEXT

1 COMPREHENSION

Decide if each sentence is correct or incorrect. If it is correct, mark A.
If it is not correct, mark B.

		A	B
1	Mary Stuart was a Protestant; she became Queen of Scots.	☐	☐
2	Mary was Elizabeth's biggest rival because many Catholics wanted her to be Queen of England.	☐	☐
3	Elizabeth was dangerously ill with smallpox but a French doctor saved her life.	☐	☐
4	Noblemen and monarchs wanted to marry Elizabeth, but she was not interested in marriage.	☐	☐
5	The Scots suspected that Mary and Lord Darnley killed the Earl of Bothwell.	☐	☐
6	Mary escaped to France and became a danger for Elizabeth.	☐	☐
7	Catholic nobles plotted against Elizabeth in favour of Mary.	☐	☐
8	Mary was imprisoned for 19 years, and in 1587 she was beheaded.	☐	☐

Now rewrite the incorrect sentences with the correct information.

2 ADJECTIVES AND NOUNS

Adjectives and nouns are often similar. Look at the example below.
Go back to Chapter Two and fill in the columns below. The first
is done for you.

NOUN	ADJECTIVE
a. happiness	happy
b. luxury	....
c.	beautiful
d. anger	....
e. fury	....
f.	dangerous

Now use the nouns or adjectives to complete the following sentences.

a. Mary Stuart was very .... in the .... French court.

b. Mary was charming and ....

c. The Scots were .... when Mary married the Earl of Bothwell.

d. Smallpox was a very .... disease.

e. Elizabeth became .... with Parliament.

 A SECRET MESSAGE
The Catholic nobles plotted against Elizabeth. Mary Queen of Scots received and sent secret messages, using a special secret code, to some of these nobles when she was in prison.
Use the key for the secret code below to read a message to Mary from one of the nobles.

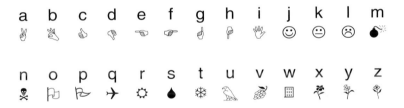

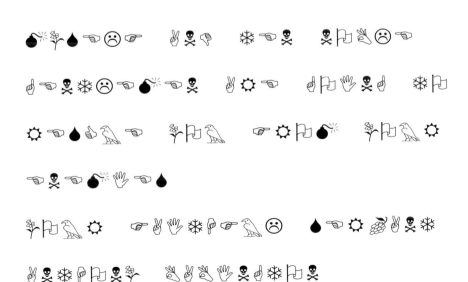

LOOKING AT THE PAINTING

Look at the painting and answer the questions.

a. Do you think the family in the painting is rich or poor? What things tell you this?

b. What animals can you see? Do you think it is strange to find these animals here?

c. How many children are there? Do you think Lord Cobham had a large family for this time?

SPEAKING

Class discussion – children

Tudor families had many children, but many of them died at birth or before the age of five.

a. What is the average number of children, per family, in your country?

b. Why do you think many children died so young in Tudor times?

Class discussion – health

Smallpox was a terrible disease. Now there is a vaccination to prevent it. We can live longer because of antibiotics and other medicines. In Tudor times not everyone was able to eat fresh fruit like the children in the painting. Today we have more information about health so we can stay healthy.

a. What modern illnesses or diseases are people afraid of? Is it possible to prevent them?

b. With another student complete the sentences below with the words *Do* or *Don't* to make a list of things we can do to keep healthy. Continue the list with your own ideas.

   1. eat a lot of fresh fruit and vegetables

     Do eat a lot of fruit and vegetables.

   2. have breakfast in the morning

   3. drink a lot of coffee

   4. eat a lot of fried food

   5. take regular exercise

William Brooke, 10th Lord Cobham and his Family, 1567 (panel),
by the Master of the Countess of Warwick.
Longleat House/Bridgeman Art Library.

CHAPTER THREE

EXPLORATION AND DISCOVERY

In 1492 Christopher Columbus, an Italian navigator who sailed from Spain, 'discovered' the New World. Now there were new countries to colonise. During the 1500s Spain and Portugal controlled sea travel on the Atlantic Ocean. England and other countries wanted to discover new trade routes to reach the Pacific Ocean. This was Elizabeth's biggest preoccupation, and she sponsored many voyages.

Spain was the richest and most powerful country in Europe. Its empire extended to the West Indies, Central and South America. Spain and Portugal shared their treasures with the Pope in Rome.

The Spanish explorers took gold, silver, jewels and other riches from the natives and transported them to Spain on their galleons. [1] Each galleon carried immense treasure.

1. **galleons** : large ships of war.

Sir Francis Drake, in the style of M. Gheeraerts (1561-1635).
National Maritime Museum, London.

Many Elizabethan captains and sailors [1] were pirates, but they were called 'privateers.' They had permission from the Queen to attack ships and take their treasure, which they shared with her. This was a common practice at that time.

Francis Drake, Sir John Hawkins and Thomas Cavendish were three famous privateers. Elizabeth affectionately called Drake 'my pirate.' Hawkins became the first Englishman to trade in [2] African slaves.

Elizabeth asked Francis Drake, an expert navigator, to sail across the South Atlantic, attack Spanish galleons and take their treasure. She also wanted him to find new trade routes.

Drake left Plymouth in 1577 on his ship *The Golden Hind* and sailed South. He attacked several Spanish galleons on the South American coast. Then he sailed up the Pacific Coast and landed in northern California in 1579. He stayed there a month and claimed [3] California for Queen Elizabeth – today this place is called Drake's Bay, California, near San Francisco. In 1936 an old metal plate was found near Drake's Bay with these words on it:

BE IT KNOWN TO ALL MEN...
JUNE 17, 1579, BY THE GRACE OF GOD AND IN THE NAME OF HER
MAJESTY QUEEN ELIZABETH OF ENGLAND...
FOREVER I TAKE POSSESSION OF THIS KINGDOM...
TO BE KNOWN UNTO ALL MEN AS NOVA ALBION.

FRANCIS DRAKE

1. **sailors** : these men work on ships at sea.
2. **trade in** : buy and sell.
3. **claimed** : said the land belonged to a specific person or country.

Exploration and Discovery

But no one knows if this metal plate was Drake's or not.

Drake then sailed across the Pacific Ocean and reached the East Indies. From there he sailed around the Cape of Good Hope and returned to England in 1580 after three long years.

Drake became the first Englishman to circumnavigate the globe. His voyage is memorable because he navigated in very difficult and dangerous conditions. He had no real maps.

Queen Elizabeth was extremely pleased with his results and knighted [1] him. She also gave him a special sword to use against England's enemies.

Drake did not only bring back immense treasures, he also brought back new foods and spices: pineapples, tomatoes,

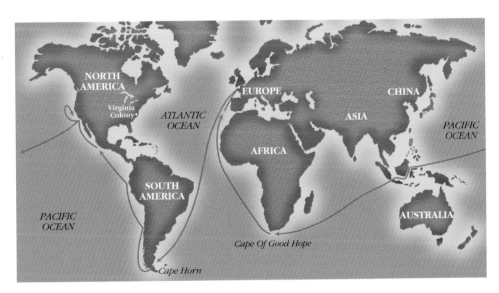

A map showing Drake's voyage, 1577-1580.

1. **knighted** : gave a title of honour: 'sir'.

bananas, coconuts, peppers and chillies. [1] Spices were very important because they preserved food and improved its taste.

English colonisation in North America began in 1584. Sir Walter Raleigh, a courageous soldier and explorer, was one of Elizabeth's favourites. He sailed to North America and set up the Virginia colony in honour of Elizabeth, the Virgin Queen.

Three years later 117 men, women and children arrived on Roanoke Island, in the Virginia colony. Living conditions were very difficult and many Indians were unfriendly. By 1590 the colony was abandoned. No one knew what happened to the colonists.

Sir Walter Raleigh brought back potatoes and tobacco from the Virginia colony. He introduced pipe smoking to the Elizabethan court and it soon became popular. This was the beginning of the tobacco trade and industry.

1. chillies :

UNDERSTANDING THE TEXT

A COMPREHENSION

Go back to the text. For each question, put a tick (✔) in the box next to the correct answer.

1. During the 1500s Spain was the most powerful country in Europe and
   - a. ☐ many Spanish captains were pirates.
   - b. ☐ it controlled sea travel on the Pacific Ocean.
   - c. ☐ its empire extended to the West Indies, Central and South America.

2. Spanish explorers
   - a. ☐ took gold, jewels and other riches from the natives.
   - b. ☐ circumnavigated the globe.
   - c. ☐ sailed to North America to set up a colony.

3. Three famous English privateers were
   - a. ☐ Drake, Hawkins and Cavendish.
   - b. ☐ Drake, Raleigh and Cavendish.
   - c. ☐ Dudley, Hawkins and Raleigh.

4. Elizabeth asked Sir Francis Drake to find new trade routes and
   - a. ☐ set up the Virginia colony.
   - b. ☐ attack Spanish galleons and take their treasures.
   - c. ☐ find tobacco and potatoes.

5. In 1579 Sir Francis Drake landed in northern California and
   - a. ☐ discovered the tobacco plant.
   - b. ☐ set up the Roanoke colony.
   - c. ☐ claimed California for Queen Elizabeth.

6. Drake circumnavigated the globe in three years and brought back
   - a. ☐ treasure, new foods and spices.
   - b. ☐ African slaves.
   - c. ☐ a metal plate from California.

7. In 1584 Sir Walter Raleigh
   - a. ☐ became a privateer.
   - b. ☐ set up the Virginia colony in North America.
   - c. ☐ discovered Nova Albion.

2 Read the descriptions and write the number of the correct answer in the box.

a. ☐ it is for smoking
b. ☐ it helps you find your way
c. ☐ it was used to fight
d. ☐ they preserve food
e. ☐ an exotic fruit
f. ☐ a precious grey metal

1. pineapple
2. spices
3. silver
4. tobacco
5. sword
6. map

3 LISTENING

Listen to this imaginary conversation between Queen Elizabeth and Sir Francis Drake. Then listen to it again and fill in the missing words.

ELIZABETH: Spain and Portugal [1].................. sea travel on the Atlantic Ocean. This is a big [2].................. . We must find a [3].................. trade route.

DRAKE: I am an expert navigator. I can sail [4].................. the ocean and discover a new trade [5].................. .

ELIZABETH: I can [6].................. for this important voyage. Take the [7].................. men and the best [8].................. . This is a [9].................. voyage. There are no [10].................. .

DRAKE: I am not [11].................. , Your Majesty. I can explore the New [12].................. and make maps. When must I [13]..................?

ELIZABETH: In November of this [14].................. . Now listen carefully.

DRAKE: Yes, Your Majesty.

ELIZABETH: You must [15].................. across the South Atlantic and [16].................. the Spanish galleons. Then take [17].................. treasure. Explore the oceans and [18].................. new trade routes, new lands and new [19].................. . Keep a diary of [20].................. you see.

DRAKE: I understand. It is an [21].................. to serve my Queen.

SPEAKING

Guess which of these types of food did not exist in Britain (or Europe) before the reign of Queen Elizabeth I. Check your answers by looking at the bottom of the page.

> cabbage   potatoes   tomatoes
> chocolate   carrots   oranges   peas

As a class, find out more about the food you eat in your country and where it came from originally. Did it arrive in your country because of the 'discovery' of other countries by explorers?

 PIRATES

Match the letters with the numbers. Then tell another student what you remember about pirates without looking at the text.

a. ☐ What do pirates do?

b. ☐ What do they look like?

c. ☐ How can you recognise a pirate ship?

d. ☐ Name a well-known book whose characters include a pirate.

1. Look for the 'Jolly Roger', a black flag with skulls, skeletons or crossbones on it.

2. They attack and rob ships at sea and they sometimes kill the crew.

3. *Treasure Island* (1883) by Robert Louis Stevenson.

4. In the past pirates wore long, dark jackets, colourful scarves and cotton shirts. Their trousers were wide and comfortable. In stories, many pirates have a patch on one eye and a wooden leg.

Potatoes and tomatoes arrived during her reign (late 1500s). Chocolate existed as a drink in Europe before her reign. It came to Britain around the early 1600s. Oranges were introduced in Medieval times. Carrots and peas had existed for a long time and cabbage is thought to be native to Britain.

CHAPTER FOUR

THE
SPANISH ARMADA

England and Spain were enemies for many years. The King of Spain, Philip II, was angry with Elizabeth for several reasons: the religious conflict was a growing problem and Philip wanted to bring the Catholic faith back to England.

For many years English pirates and privateers attacked Spanish galleons and took their rich treasure. This exasperated Philip.

In 1585 Elizabeth sent an army to help Dutch Protestants fight the Spanish. When Mary Stuart was beheaded, Philip was furious. He decided to invade England and take the throne from Elizabeth. The Pope strongly supported his plan.

The Spanish Armada had about 130 big ships and about 28,000 men. It was commanded by the Duke of Medina Sidonia. Elizabeth knew about Philip's plan. She ordered her best captains, Sir Francis Drake, John Hawkins and Martin Frobisher, to prepare for the attack.

The Spanish Armada

England had a powerful navy of about 160 smaller ships and about 14,000 men. It was commanded by Lord Howard of Effingham, one of Elizabeth's cousins.

In 1587 Drake attacked 30 Spanish galleons by surprise in Cadiz, Spain. 'I have singed [1] the King of Spain's beard,' he said proudly. His brilliant action pleased Elizabeth and hurt the Spanish.

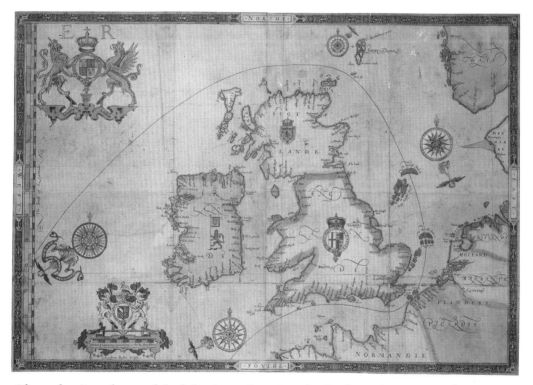

Chart showing the track [2] of the Armada, 1588, by Rythier, Augustine after Adams, R.
National Maritime Museum, London.

---

1. **singed** [sɪnʒd] : burned.
2. **track** : route.

Elizabeth did not like war, but she was determined to defend England. Before the Spanish attack she visited her army and said,

Launch of Fireships Against the Armada, by an artist of the Netherlandish School, 16th century.
National Maritime Museum, London.

The Spanish Armada

'I have the body of a weak... woman, but I have the heart and stomach of a king!' She was a courageous woman.

In July 1588 the impressive Armada sailed up the English Channel. The weather was against the Spanish. The English attacked at Plymouth, using new tactics to surprise the enemy. After several sea battles the Armada reached Calais (see map on page 69).

Lord Howard sent eight fireships [1] to Calais. When the Spanish saw them they were terrified and immediately left the port. There were other sea battles and both countries fought courageously. In the end the Armada was badly defeated [2] and returned to Spain with only 67 ships. This was a glorious victory for England, but it was a disaster for Spain. After this defeat, Spain slowly lost its sea power.

By 1590 Elizabeth was almost 60 years old. She was still healthy and energetic, but her aspect changed. She wore a red wig [3] and her face was covered with heavy white make-up. Her teeth were in very bad condition. However, she was still vain. Every morning she spent more than two hours getting ready. [4] She had about 3,000 magnificent dresses and innumerable splendid jewels. She was always very careful with her personal hygiene, and took a bath once a month. She hated bad odours and loud noise.

Elizabeth's court was a centre for playwrights, [5] artists and musicians. Edmund Spenser's famous poem, *The Faerie Queen*, was dedicated to Elizabeth.

1. **fireships** : burning ships sent to burn and destroy enemy ships.
2. **defeated** : lost the battle or war.
3. **wig** : artificial hair.
4. **getting ready** : preparing herself.
5. **playwrights** : these people write plays.

The Spanish Armada

English drama flourished [1] during this period. William Shakespeare was born on 23 April 1564 in Stratford-upon-Avon. His father was a glove-maker. [2] He attended school at Stratford until he was fifteen.

When he was eighteen he married Anne Hathaway; they had three children.

He went to London in about 1587, before the sea battle of the Spanish Armada. With England's brilliant victory over the Armada, the great English literary Renaissance began and Shakespeare became the most famous English writer of all time.

William Shakespeare.

In London he worked as an actor and began to write plays and poetry. By 1592 William Shakespeare was famous in London. His plays were very successful and he became a rich man. He wrote 38 tragedies, comedies and historical plays. Some of his best known plays are *Hamlet*, *Macbeth*, *The Merchant of Venice*, *A Midsummer Night's Dream* and *Romeo and Juliet*. He and his group often performed for Queen Elizabeth and her court.

People of all social classes started going to the theatre. In London open air theatres became very popular. Shakespeare's spectators were a noisy crowd. They talked, laughed, shouted, ate and drank during the performances. In open air theatres plays

1. **flourished** : grew successfully
2. **glove-maker** : this person makes:

began in the afternoon when there was plenty of light. When it rained many of the spectators got wet. Women's roles were played by young men, because women did not act in the theatre. Shakespeare's plays were performed at the Globe, the Swan and the Rose Theatres.

Shakespeare died on his birthday in 1616 and was buried in Stratford-upon-Avon. (The Globe Theatre was recently rebuilt so you can enjoy Shakespeare's plays on the original site in London.)

Other important Elizabethan playwrights were Christopher Marlowe and Ben Jonson.

Elizabeth's last favourite was the handsome Earl of Essex. She loved him dearly, although he was 34 years younger than her. She made him a military leader, but he betrayed her. He was accused of treason and beheaded in 1601.

In 1603 Elizabeth was 70 years old. She ate very little and was weak. She died on March 24, 1603, and was the last Tudor monarch. She named James VI of Scotland, the son of Mary Stuart, heir to the throne. Her people mourned her for a long time.

Her reign lasted 44 years. Under Elizabeth trade grew, Spain was defeated, and England became a European power.

UNDERSTANDING THE TEXT

⚠ COMPREHENSION

Go back to the text. For each question, put a tick (✔) in the box next to the correct answer.

1. Who was angry with Queen Elizabeth?
   - a. ☐ Edmund Spenser
   - b. ☐ the Dutch Protestants
   - c. ☐ King Philip of Spain

2. Who decided to invade England and take the throne from Elizabeth?
   - a. ☐ Lord Howard of Effingham
   - b. ☐ King Philip of Spain
   - c. ☐ Duke Medina Sidonia

3. How many ships and men were there in the Spanish Armada?
   - a. ☐ 130 ships and about 28,000 men
   - b. ☐ 197 ships and about 15,000 men
   - c. ☐ 183 ships and about 15,000 men

4. What terrified the Spanish in Calais?
   - a. ☐ the English army
   - b. ☐ eight fireships
   - c. ☐ the powerful English navy

5. What happened to the Spanish Armada?
   - a. ☐ It was victorious.
   - b. ☐ It was destroyed at Calais.
   - c. ☐ It was defeated.

6. Who is the greatest English writer?
   - a. ☐ William Shakespeare
   - b. ☐ Ben Jonson
   - c. ☐ Christopher Marlowe

7. The Globe, the Swan and the Rose were
   - a. ☐ plays written by Shakespeare.
   - b. ☐ open-air theatres in London.
   - c. ☐ characters in Shakespeare's plays.

SUMMARY

Put the following sentences in chronological order. One is done for you.

a. ☐ When Queen Mary died Elizabeth became Queen of England.

b. ☐1☐ Elizabeth was born. She was the daughter of Henry VIII and Anne Boleyn.

c. ☐ Sir Walter Raleigh set up the Virginia colony in North America.

d. ☐ The English Navy defeated the Spanish Armada.

e. ☐ Mary Stuart, Elizabeth's cousin and a dangerous rival, was beheaded.

f. ☐ Sir Francis Drake returned to England after his circumnavigation of the globe and brought back a lot of treasure and new foods.

g. ☐ When Elizabeth died she named James VI of Scotland heir to the throne.

QUIZ

Famous Elizabethans

We call people born at the time of Elizabeth I 'Elizabethans'. Use a Web encyclopaedia to find out about these famous Elizabethans and then do the quiz.

1. Christopher Marlowe wrote
   a. *Macbeth.*   b. *Dr Faustus.*   c. *The Canterbury Tales.*

2. Which of these places is not connected to Sir Walter Raleigh's life?
   a. El Dorado   b. the Tower of London   c. New England

3. As well as plays Shakespeare also wrote
   a. poetry.   b. novels.   c. historical books.

4. Robert Devereux, Earl of Essex, was famous in Elizabeth's court as
   a. an adventurous explorer.   b. a man of great education.
   c. a brave soldier.

5. Which of these places did Sir Francis Drake reach?
   a. China   b. the Panama Canal   c. the North Pole

1. b.   2. c.   3. a.   4. c.   5. b

KEY

76

'Reading' a Painting

The Armada Portrait was painted to celebrate England's victory over the Spanish Armada in 1588. Smaller and faster ships were victorious over the powerful, big galleons. The sea was England's best ally: many Spanish ships were destroyed by storms [1] at sea. In this painting two different moments of the sea battle can be seen in the background. A day scene represents the Spanish galleons advancing on a calm sea, confident of victory. The night scene shows the defeat of the Armada in the English Channel.

In the foreground you can see Queen Elizabeth I. She was considered almost a divinity by her people and her portraits are similar to holy [2] images. Her face is eternally young and there are no shadows on it. Elizabeth controlled her own image. No painting or drawing representing her circulated without her permission. This explains why in all her portraits she looks 'frozen' at more or less the same

1. **storms** : very bad weather with wind and rain.
2. **holy** : religious.

age and never looks older. The Queen's magnificent gown is made of velvet and silk. It is decorated with pearls and gold. Every ribbon on her gown is decorated with a precious stone.

Elizabeth's hand is on the globe. Her fingers are touching America, where Sir Walter Raleigh established the Virginia colony. He called it Virginia in honour of Queen Elizabeth, the Virgin Queen. A small statue of a sea creature is near her left hand. In this painting she is the ruler of both earth and sea.

When you 'read' this portrait you can see that the Elizabethan painters were not interested in naturalism. They did not depict [1] reality in their paintings, as artists in the Italian Renaissance at that time did (think of paintings by Leonardo, Raphael and Michelangelo). English painters preferred to use symbols in their works.

1. **depict** : (here) reproduce, show.

'The Armada Portrait' of Queen Elizabeth I, by George Gower (c. 1588) Woburn Abbey.
By kind permission of the Marquess of Tavistock and the Trustees of the Bedford Estate.

LOOKING AT THE PAINTING
Look at the painting and answer the questions.

1. In the background there are two representations of the Armada. Which one shows the voyage and which one shows the defeat of the Spanish fleet?
   a. voyage ☐ the one to the left ☐ the one to the right
   b. defeat ☐ the one to the left ☐ the one to the right

2. Do you think this portrait shows Elizabeth as she really was? Why?/Why not?

3. The face of the Queen is
   a. happy   b. sad   c. without expression

4. What is on the left of the Queen? Why do you think the artist painted it here?
   a. To show Elizabeth was the Queen, but she had too many jewels in her hair to wear it.
   b. To show the importance of royal power.
   c. To show that the ships fought in the name of the ruler of England.

 SPEAKING – BEAUTY
In Elizabethan times pale skin was thought to be a sign of beauty. Many women used white face powder so their skin looked pale. They also wanted to look thinner. They wore very tight, uncomfortable pieces of clothing called corsets.
Think about the things people do to make themselves beautiful today and discuss the questions with another student.

a. What do people do to make themselves beautiful today?
b. What do you think makes someone beautiful?

3 **Find a picture of Queen Elizabeth II. Compare it to the picture of Queen Elizabeth I. Think about:**

a. their clothes
b. their facial expressions
c. the background of the pictures

PART THREE

Victoria — Mother of the Empire

Queen Victoria (1875), by Heinrich von Angeli.
The Royal Collection © 1999, Her Majesty Queen Elizabeth II.

Introduction

Queen Victoria reigned longer than any other British Monarch: 63 years. She was an honest, highly dedicated monarch and was dearly loved by her people. During her reign Britain became the richest and most powerful nation in the world.

The Victorian Age was a time of great change in the way people lived and worked. The train replaced the stage-coach [1] and electricity was used for lights. It was also a time of exceptional achievements [2] in science and industry.

In other parts of the world photography, cars and telephones were invented. Victoria was the first monarch who was photographed.

Charles Dickens, Emily and Charlotte Brontë, Robert Louis Stevenson, Oscar Wilde and other great writers created their masterpieces [3] during the Victorian Age.

The British Empire grew and expanded around the world. It became so vast [4] that 'the sun never set on it'.

Commerce and industry prospered, [5] and created a lot of wealth. People moved from the country to industrial towns and cities to work in factories. This was the beginning of the Industrial Age.

1. **stage-coach** :
2. **achievements** : progress.
3. **masterpieces** : (here) great works of literature.
4. **vast** : very big, enormous.
5. **prospered** : were very successful.

CHAPTER ONE

THE LONELY PRINCESS

On 24 May 1819 a little princess was born at Kensington Palace in London. Her name was Alexandrina Victoria. She was the daughter of the Duke of Kent, King William's brother, and a German Princess, Victoria of Saxe-Coburg.

Victoria's father died when she was a baby. Her childhood was lonely and dull. [1] She had no friends to play with. Her favourite toys were dolls. She rarely went out because her mother was very protective. She grew up with her mother and her strict German governess, Baroness Lehzen. Victoria adored Baroness Lehzen.

Victoria later wrote that she 'had no brothers or sisters to live with – never had a father, and did not know what a happy home life was.'

The young Princess loved animals and had three pets: a dog

---

1. **dull** : boring, not interesting.

called Dash, a canary and a parakeet. [1] She had private lessons in many subjects from half past nine in the morning to six in the evening. She loved singing and dancing.

At the age of twelve Victoria said, 'I see I am nearer the throne than I supposed.' On that day she made a promise, 'I will be good.'

When Victoria was 13 her mother decided that she must see Britain and that the British people must see her. The young Princess travelled to Wales, the Midlands, Yorkshire and the south coast. She was welcomed with enthusism everywhere. These journeys were not a holiday but a part of her education.

Victoria wrote about her journey in her diary. She did not know that thousands of poor children worked in factories and mills [2] in terrible conditions. They never went to school and often died at a young age. She also learned that working people lived in small, dark houses and were often hungry.

On Victoria's seventeenth birthday her German cousin, Prince Albert, came to visit her. Victoria liked him immediately. Her mother thought Prince Albert was the ideal husband and Victoria agreed.

At five in the morning on 20 June 1837 Victoria received the news: King William IV died that night and she was now the Queen. She was only eighteen and knew very little about government or politics. At half past eleven that morning she went to meet her advisers, the Privy Councillors. [3] She spoke and behaved calmly, and everyone admired her.

1. **parakeet** :
2. **mills** : (here) factories where textiles and steel are made.
3. **Privy Councillors** : these important advisers counsel a monarch.

The Lonely Princess

The young Queen now lived at Buckingham Palace, away from the strict control of her mother. Victoria enjoyed going to the opera and the ballet, and began horse riding. Since she was short (almost 5 foot = 1.5 metres) she felt taller on a horse.

Lord Melbourne, the Prime Minister, was the most important person in Victoria's early years as Queen. He was a kind and loyal friend. He gave her advice and helped her understand politics and government.

In 1839 Victoria's cousin, Albert, visited her again. This is what she wrote in her diary: 'Albert really is quite charming, and so excessively handsome. My heart is quite going.' [1] Victoria loved Albert and proposed to him. (Albert could not propose because he was of lower rank.)

They were married in 1840. Victoria and Albert loved each

An 1837 handbill asking Londoners to celebrate Victoria's 18th birthday.

1. **quite going** : beating fast.

other very much. She called him 'an angel.' However, Albert was a foreigner [1] and not everyone liked him. Parliament did not give Albert a title and many Londoners said rude [2] things about him.

Albert was intelligent, well-educated and responsible. He was very interested in science, music and the arts. Victoria learned from Albert to be a dedicated monarch. The Queen asked for his help on government affairs, and they always worked together.

Queen Victoria and Prince Albert, 30th June 1854.
The Royal Archives © 1999, Her Majesty Queen Elizabeth II.

1. **foreigner** : this person comes from another country.
2. **rude** : not polite.

UNDERSTANDING THE TEXT

COMPREHENSION

Go back to the text. Circle the correct word.
Now listen and check your answers.

a. Victoria's childhood was *lively / lonely*. She grew up with her *mother / father* and her German *governor / governess*.

b. When Victoria was *30 / 13* she visited *parts / past* of Britain, and *wrote / rode* about her journey in her *dairy / diary*.

c. Victoria *became / becomes* Queen when she was 18 *years / ears* old.

d. Lord Melbourne helped Victoria *understanding / understand* politics and *governor / government*.

e. Victoria loved Albert and *day / they* were *marry / married* in February 1840.

f. Not everyone liked Albert *because / became* he was a *foreign / foreigner*.

g. Albert was *negligent / intelligent* and responsible. Victoria learned from *him / his* to be a *delicate / dedicated* monarch.

LANGUAGE

*She **rarely** went out.*

> ***How often** do you go out with your friends at the weekend?*
> We often answer this question using an **adverb of frequency**.
> This is a word we use to speak about how often we do something.
> Adverbs of frequency come **before** the main verb in a sentence, but they come **after** the verb 'to be'.
>
> | never | rarely/hardly ever | sometimes | often | usually | always |
> |---|---|---|---|---|---|
>
> 0%   100%
>
> *I **always** go out with my friends on Saturday night. We **usually** meet outside a café. I am **often** late.*

Princess Victoria was not allowed to go out with her friends. There are many things that ordinary people do that the royal family probably cannot do, and vice versa. With a partner list as many examples as you can. Use adjectives of frequency from the language box.

Example: I often have to do the washing up after dinner. Prince William probably never has to do the washing up.

Now rewrite these sentences with an adverb of frequency to make true sentences about yourself.

Example:
I go to the cinema during the week. I often go the cinema during the week.
a. I eat breakfast before going to school/work.
b. I play games on the computer at home/work.
c. I go out dancing at the weekend.
d. I make dinner for other people.
e. I tidy my room/my flat.

 At the age of 13 the young princess travelled around England and Wales to see more of the country. Go back to the text to find the places she visited and mark them on the map.

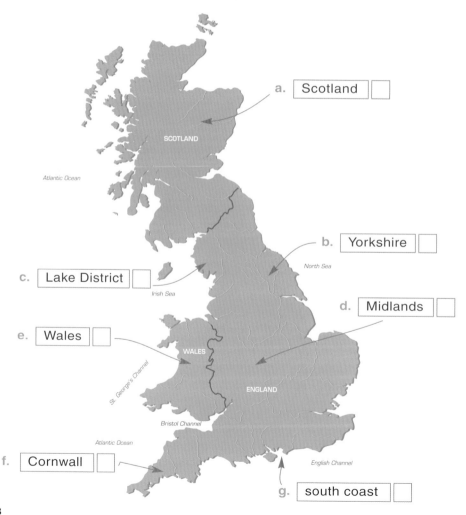

5 Here is a page from young Victoria's diary. Unscramble the words and put the verbs in the Past Simple.

Midlands, April 15, 1832

This *nrgmoin* I (visit) .... a town with a *gbi* factory. I (be)
.... very *sdupsreir*!
I (see) .... small, dark *suehos* and dirty *etestrs*. A *myafli* of eight
people (live) .... in *neo* room! They (be) .... very *orpo*,
hungry and *dsa*.
Then I (go) .... to see the *yatcofr*. *Yamn* children (work) ....
there. They (do) .... dangerous *rwok*. They (do) .... not
have any shoes on their *tefe* and it (be) .... very cold.
There (be) .... no *hoscol* in the town. What a sad *yad*!

6 VOCABULARY
Match these words and expressions to their definitions.

a. ☐ relationship
b. ☐ dating agency
c. ☐ arranged marriage
d. ☐ get married
e. ☐ a good match

1. to become someone's husband or wife
2. when other people choose a person for you to marry
3. when two people have the right character to be together
4. a romantic friendship with someone
5. this business arranges for people to meet each other

7 SPEAKING
Class discussion – arranged marriages
Royal marriages were usually arranged for political reasons.
But Queen Victoria's family allowed her to marry someone of a lower status because they knew it was a good match.
What do you think about arranged marriages? Discuss these questions with another student.

a. What do you know about the marriages of the British royal family today? Do you think the royal family can choose the person they want to be their wife/husband?
b. Do you think someone else (e.g. a dating agency, friends, relatives) can find the best match for a person?
c. Do you think your parents' opinion about a boyfriend/girlfriend is important? What about your friends' advice?

CHAPTER TWO

THE GROWTH OF COMMERCE AND INDUSTRY

I n November 1840 the Queen had her first child, Victoria. She was very clever and was the Queen's favourite child. In 1841 Albert Edward, Prince of Wales, was born.

Between 1840 and 1857 Victoria and Albert had nine children – four sons and five daughters. Victoria was a strict [1] mother. The children's food and clothing were always very simple. Victoria and Albert were devoted parents and spent a lot of time with their children. Family values and morality were very important to the royal couple. They became an example for their people. Most Victorians had large families. In the late 1800s, the average family had five or six children.

1. **strict** : severe.

The Growth of Commerce and Industry

Albert introduced the first Christmas tree to the royal family, since it was a German custom. Soon it was popular all over Britain. Victoria was very fond of Christmas and its traditions.

The first public railway opened in 1825 and attracted a lot of attention. It was built by George Stephenson, an engineer. In 1830 the Liverpool to Manchester Railway opened and soon transported 1200 passengers every day.

With the railway, people and goods travelled cheaply and quickly. Railways spread [1] rapidly all over England, Scotland and Wales. People started going to the seaside, and seaside towns developed. By 1848 there were no more stage coaches – almost everyone travelled by train.

The Royal Family at Osborne, May 1857.
The Royal Archives © 1999, Her Majesty Queen Elizabeth II.

1. **spread** : grew in all directions.

Great English
MONARCHS
and their Times

In 1842 Victoria and Albert took their first train ride. The Queen liked the speed, comfort and privacy of the train. Soon the royal family travelled by the Royal Train, in a specially designed carriage. In 1840 the first national postal system was created and the 'Penny Black' became the first adhesive postage stamp. Victoria's profile appeared on it. It cost only one penny to send a letter anywhere in Great Britain. Today the red Victorian letter boxes are still used.

Victoria had three royal houses but she didn't like any of them. She wanted a private, remote family home. She and Albert bought a large estate [1] called Osborne on the Isle of Wight. Victoria loved Osborne and was very happy there.

In 1847 the royal couple bought a house in Scotland: Balmoral Castle. It was surrounded [2] by green hills and forests. Victoria liked the fresh, clean air and Albert liked hunting and fishing.

Poverty was a big problem in 19th-century Britain. Working people had a very difficult life. Adults and children worked long hours in factories in dangerous conditions. They were usually hungry and often ill. Squalid houses, unclean water and dirty streets caused many diseases. The air was full of smoke and fog. People did not live long in these conditions.

People without work lived on the streets. They were beggars [3] or thieves. Others lived in workhouses. [4] Some Victorians tried to help the poor. Dr Barnardo opened a home for orphans in London.

---

1. **estate** : large piece of land in the country with a house on it.
2. **surrounded** : enclosed on all sides.
3. **beggars** : these poor people ask others for money or food.
4. **workhouses** : places where poor people did unpleasant jobs in return for food and accommodation.

The Growth of Commerce and Industry

Charles Dickens wrote about these social problems in his novels, for example in *Oliver Twist* and *David Copperfield*.

Social reforms were seriously needed. In 1847 the Ten Hour Act limited the working day of women and children to ten hours a day.

In 1848 Parliament passed laws to make towns and cities cleaner. But progress was very slow.

The middle and upper classes had clean, comfortable houses, far from the industrial centres, in green areas called suburbs. Their children received a good education.

Children at work.

Under Victoria's reign Britain became the richest commercial nation. It produced machines, textiles, ships and other goods, and sold them to other countries.

Albert wanted to show Britain's products, inventions and machines to the world. He decided to open an international exhibition. For two years he worked intensely on this complex project. The British began to appreciate Albert's qualities.

On 1 May 1851 Queen Victoria opened the Great Exhibition in the Crystal Palace in London. She called it 'the most beautiful spectacle ever seen.' The Crystal Palace was truly a spectacle. It was made of iron and glass, and was as big as four football fields. There were over 7,000 exhibitors from Britain and 6,000 from other countries. It was an enormous success with over 6 million visitors in 140 days.

The Inauguration of the Great Exhibition, 1 May 1851, by David Roberts (1796-1864).

UNDERSTANDING THE TEXT

COMPREHENSION

Decide if each sentence is correct or incorrect. If it is correct, mark A. If it is not correct, mark B.

		A	B
1	Victoria and Albert had nine children, but they spent little time with them.	☐	☐
2	People liked the railway because it was fast and cheap.	☐	☐
3	The Penny Black was the name of the first public railway.	☐	☐
4	Osborne and Balmoral Castle were the royal couple's favourite homes.	☐	☐
5	Charles Dickens wrote about the social problems of the Victorian Age in his novels.	☐	☐
6	The Ten Hour Act made education free for all.	☐	☐
7	There were more than 13,000 exhibitors at the Great Exhibition in London.	☐	☐

Rewrite the incorrect sentences with the correct information.

T: GRADE 4

Topic – Holidays

When the railways were built, people started travelling to the seaside and seaside resorts like Brighton (see photo) developed. Today air travel means that people can go abroad for their holidays. Find a photo or some information about a holiday destination you have been to and then discuss the questions with a partner.

a. Where do you and your family normally go on holiday?

b. When did you last go to this place? How did you travel there?

c. Which places are popular holiday resorts in/outside your country today?

CROSSWORD PUZZLE

Across

1. The streets of London were full of ... and fog.

2.

3. [train image]

4. Victoria's estate on the Isle of Wight.

5. Victorian writer.

6. Prince Albert was ... .

7. Green areas far from the centre of the city.

Down

8. The Queen's first child.

9. Balmoral Castle is in ... .

10. Victorian letter boxes are ... .

11. Poor person who asks for food or money.

12. The Crystal Palace was made of iron and ... .

4 **Read the text about the Industrial Revolution. For each question, mark the letter next to the correct word – A, B, C or D.**

The Industrial Revolution

The Industrial Revolution changed society in a (0) ..B... way and in a (1) ...... space of time.

Before the Industrial Revolution people mostly worked (2) ...... the land. Goods were made in small groups of houses. New technological inventions helped to build new, bigger machines. These machines could (3) ...... large quantities of goods and used less people to produce them. This started a new age. Factories were built and people moved from the countryside to (4) ...... and work in the cities.

The industrial age brought (5) ...... goods and new wealth, but lots of people became unemployed as a result. There was also not (6) ...... housing for the workers.

Today industry is developing in new areas of the world. Some of these new developments have brought pollution and big changes (7) ...... natural habitats.

0	A very	B big	C large	D interesting
1	A short	B no	C big	D little
2	A in	B at	C of	D on
3	A do	B make	C did	D made
4	A stayed	B be	C live	D went
5	A cheapest	B most	C a lot	D cheaper
6	A same	B enough	C many	D old
7	A of	B with	C to	D at

PROJECT **ON THE WEB**

Your teacher will give you the correct web-site address. Find out more about the Industrial Revolution. Answer these questions then discuss your answers with another student.

a. When did the Industrial Revolution begin in Britain? What about in your country?

b. Which cities grew during the Industrial Revolution in Britain? Which cities are industrial centres in your country? What are the main industries there?

c. Name four main changes as a result of the Industrial Revolution.

CHAPTER THREE

WARS AND LOSS

During the 1850s there were wars and revolts in Europe and Asia. British soldiers fought in several of them. The most important was the Crimean War on the Black Sea. Russia wanted to expand its empire and perhaps block the Mediterranean and overland routes to India. So Britain and France decided to help Turkey fight Russia.

The Crimean War (1854-6) was the first war that was photographed. For the first time newspapers showed photographs of a war – a painful, tragic spectacle.

Victoria was very unhappy because the soldiers suffered. She sent them mittens [1] and scarves, and visited the wounded [2] soldiers in British hospitals. She wrote letters to the soldiers' widows. Albert wrote hundreds of letters to Members of Parliament to ask them to send more help to the soldiers.

1. **mittens** :
2. **wounded** : injured.

Victoria helped Florence Nightingale, [1] who went to Crimea with 38 nurses. She courageously set up a hospital for wounded soldiers and saved many lives. After the war Florence Nightingale opened the first school for nurses in London. This was the beginning of modern nursing and improved hygienic conditions in hospitals.

When the Crimean War ended in 1856 Victoria presented a special medal for courage to many soldiers. This medal was called the Victoria Cross and it was made of a captured Russian cannon.

Victoria Cross.

At this time India was controlled by the British East India Company, a trading company set up [2] in India. In 1857 there was a rebellion against the British who lived in India. It was called the Indian Mutiny. Thousands of people were killed. After this rebellion India became part of the British Empire and was controlled by the British government.

Victoria was very healthy and was rarely ill. She did not like hot rooms and always kept windows open, even in winter.

Albert was usually cold and was not as healthy as Victoria. He worked too much and rarely rested. He was also worried about his son, the Prince of Wales. The Prince's adventures with women

---

1. **Florence Nightingale** : (1820-1910) – today her name is synonymous with modern nursing.
2. **set up** : established.

Wars and Loss

and gambling [1] shocked Albert, who was very upright. [2]

Albert became very tired and weak. In November 1861 he caught typhoid fever, but he continued working until he died on 14 December. Victoria was devastated – it was the greatest agony of her life. She was lost without Albert. She was convinced that her son, the Prince of Wales, was responsible for Albert's death. She did not permit the Prince of Wales to help her with government work.

Victoria visited Albert's impressive tomb at Frogmore near Windsor regularly. She wanted everyone to remember him. The Albert Memorial and the Royal Albert Hall near the Kensington Gardens in London were built to honour her beloved husband.

In her sadness and misery Victoria became a recluse. For thirteen years she refused to appear in public and go to Privy Council meetings. However, she continued studying government papers privately and never lost contact with her kingdom. She spent a lot of time at Balmoral Castle,

The Albert Memorial, London.

---

1. **gambling** : playing cards or other games for money.
2. **upright** : virtuous, honest.

far from London. A Scottish servant called John Brown became her loyal friend.

During this period Victoria and the monarchy became very unpopular, and some politicians wanted to abolish it and create a republic.

Queen Victoria on Fyrie, attended by J. Brown (left) and J. Grant, Balmoral, October 1863.
The Royal Archives © 1999, Her Majesty Queen Elizabeth II.

UNDERSTANDING THE TEXT

> ⚠️ **COMPREHENSION**
> **Go back to the text. For each question, put a tick (✔) in the box next to the correct answer.**

1. During the Crimean War, Britain and France
   a. ☐ helped Turkey to fight Russia.
   b. ☐ expanded their empires.
   c. ☐ fought against India.

2. After the Crimean War Florence Nightingale
   a. ☐ opened a hospital in London.
   b. ☐ opened the first school for nurses.
   c. ☐ became a doctor.

3. The Victoria Cross was
   a. ☐ an impressive monument in Windsor.
   b. ☐ a special medal for courage at war.
   c. ☐ the name of Florence Nightingale's hospital in Crimea.

4. After the Indian Mutiny of 1857
   a. ☐ the British East India Company left India.
   b. ☐ India became an independent nation.
   c. ☐ India became part of the British Empire.

5. Albert was not as healthy as Victoria and in November 1861 he
   a. ☐ caught typhoid fever.
   b. ☐ went to live in Scotland.
   c. ☐ consulted several German doctors.

6. Victoria was devastated by Albert's death and
   a. ☐ became very ill.
   b. ☐ went to live at Frogmore near Windsor.
   c. ☐ became a recluse.

7. During this period some politicians wanted
   a. ☐ to abolish the monarchy and create a republic.
   b. ☐ a new queen.
   c. ☐ a new prime minister.

2 WHO DID WHAT?

Who:

a. was very upright? ....

b. liked gambling? ....

c. wrote letters to the soldiers' widows? ....

d. went to Crimea with 38 nurses? ....

e. received the Victoria Cross? ....

f. was Victoria's loyal friend at Balmoral Castle? ....

g. wanted to abolish the monarchy? ....

h. was rarely ill? ....

i. died of typhoid fever? ....

j. opened the first school for nurses in London? ....
   ....

3 In Chapter Three there a lot of words to describe sadness and suffering. Go back to the text and underline the ones you can find.

4 Now complete these sentences with a word from the text.

a. The Queen was .... about the suffering of the soldiers in the Crimean War.

b. The pictures from the Crimean War showed how tragic and .... war really is.

c. Florence Nightingale saved the lives of many .... soldiers.

d. Victoria was .... by her husband's death.

e. The loss of her husband, Albert, was a great .... for Victoria.

f. The Queen refused to appear in public and became almost a recluse in her sadness and ....

CHAPTER FOUR

THE END OF AN ERA

I n 1866 Victoria opened Parliament for the first time after Albert's death. She was dressed in black, the colour of mourning, which she wore for the rest of her life.

Transportation became a big problem in London because roads were always crowded. In 1863 the first underground railway in the world opened in London. Today it is called the 'tube'.

This was a period of social reforms. In 1870 the Education Act was passed. It introduced the first state schools for all children between the ages of five and thirteen.

Factory reforms, new laws for the poor and new hospitals improved people's lives. In 1875 many slums [1] were destroyed and better homes were built. However, poverty was still a big problem.

In 1878 the American inventor Alexander Bell showed the Queen his invention, the telephone.

---

1. **slums** : city areas of poor, dirty, broken houses.

The poor people of London.

Victoria was astonished. She was even more astonished to learn about the invention of a new means of transport, the automobile.

This was a period of revolutionary change.

At this time Victoria's favourite Prime Minister was Benjamin Disraeli, a witty, intelligent man. He got along well with [1] the Queen and encouraged her to return to public life.

Disraeli wanted to expand the British Empire. His political rival, William Gladstone, wanted to limit it. Victoria did not like Gladstone. He complained about the cost of the Albert Memorial.

Victoria liked Disraeli's idea of a bigger and stronger British Empire. In 1869 the Suez Canal, built by the French, opened and created an important trade route to India and the East. Great Britain bought shares [2] in the

---

1. **got along well with** : worked well with.
2. **shares** : documents you buy that make you part-owner of a business; investment in a business.

canal to secure Britain's power in the East.

India was an important colony with its production of tea, silk and cotton. Victoria was fascinated by India and was delighted to become Empress of India in 1876. The British Empire expanded rapidly with the addition of Borneo, Burma and New Guinea (see map on page 109).

David Livingstone was a British missionary and a great explorer. In the 1850s he travelled extensively in Africa and made the first maps of Central Africa. He discovered six lakes, rivers,

Benjamin Disraeli.

mountains and the biggest waterfall in the world, called Victoria Falls in honour of the Queen. Henry Morton Stanley explored Lake Tanganyika and the Congo River.

In the 1880s Britain took control of large parts of Africa: Egypt, Nigeria, Kenya and Uganda. In 1883 there was a war in Sudan and rebels destroyed the British command in Khartoum. From its African colonies Britain got cocoa, coffee and diamonds.

On 20 June 1887 Victoria celebrated her 50 years as Queen. The following day she rode through London in an open carriage [1] for the spectacular Golden Jubilee celebrations. The streets were full of cheering [2] people.

1. **carriage** :

2. **cheering** : shouting to show they are happy.

A procession of royal guests [1] from all over the world rode in front of Victoria. There were Kings and Queens from Europe, the Crown Prince of Prussia and Princes from India, Japan and Siam. [2] Victoria was very fond of music and liked singing arias from the comic operas of Gilbert and Sullivan. [3] *The Mikado, The Pirates of Penzance* and *HMS Pinafore* are their most famous

Escort of Indian Cavalry passing the Houses of Parliament, June 22nd 1897.
The Royal Archives © 1999, Her Majesty Queen Elizabeth II.

1. **guests** : these people are invited to an event.
2. **Siam** : the old name for Thailand.
3. **Gilbert and Sullivan** : a famous English musical team. They wrote comic operas.

The End of an Era

operas. However, it was the famous British composer Edward Elgar who wrote music for the great celebration.

But Victoria felt sad and lonely. 'I sat alone,' she wrote, 'Oh! without my beloved husband!' All of her children married into royal families in different parts of Europe.

When Victoria celebrated her Diamond Jubilee in 1897 there was another gigantic procession, with 50,000 troops from all over the British Empire. On that day Victoria pressed a button to send a telegraph message around the empire: 'From my heart I thank my beloved people. May God bless them!'

In 1899 the British Empire was the biggest empire in the

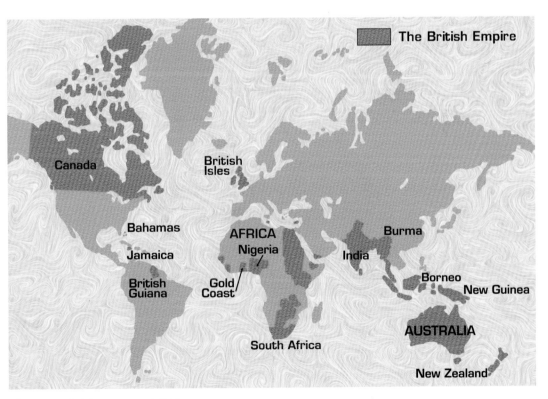

The British Empire in 1899.

world. It covered one-fifth of the earth's land area with 370 million people (see map page on 109).

Victoria was now an old woman and suffered from rheumatism. She could not walk well but she was still active. She worked from half past seven in the morning until late at night, studying government papers. She loved her people and her empire.

At the beginning of 1901 the Queen was very weak. On 22 January 1901 Victoria died at the age of 82 at Osborne House. Thousands of people wept [1] during her funeral procession. She was considered the Mother of the British Empire. She was buried beside her beloved Albert at Frogmore near Windsor.

Queen Victoria, c. 1882.
The Royal Archives © 1999,
Her Majesty Queen Elizabeth II.

1. **wept** : past simple of verb 'to weep', to cry.

UNDERSTANDING THE TEXT

⚠ COMPREHENSION

Fill in the gaps with the words in the box.

> India   diamonds   'tube'   automobile   missionary
> colony   telephone   railway   coffee   land   Disraeli
> cotton   expand   Golden Jubilee   Africa
> social reforms   Suez Canal   biggest   Empress   silk

a. The .... in London was the first underground ....
   in the world.

b. In the 1870s there were several .... to help
   the poor.

c. Victoria was astonished by the invention of the .... and the
   ....

d. Victoria got along well with .... , who wanted to
   .... the British Empire.

e. The British government bought control of the ....
   .... , which opened an important trade route to
   ....

f. India was an important .... , and it produced tea,
   .... and ....

g. In 1876 Victoria became .... of India and the British Empire
   expanded rapidly.

h. David Livingstone was a British .... and explorer who made
   maps of ....

i. Britain got cocoa, ... and .... from Africa.

j. There were kings and queens from all over the world at Victoria's
   ....

k. In 1899 the British Empire was the .... empire in the world
   and covered one-fifth of the earth's .... area.

2 Find the names of the important people in Chapter Four and put them in the correct category. Then add any more you know from that period.

Politicians	Explorers	Inventors	Musicians

What did the explorers explore? ....

What did the inventors invent? ....

What did the musicians compose? ....

3 SPEAKING

Class discussion – inventions

a. In your opinion, what was the most important invention of the 19th century?

b. Name five important inventions of the 20th century and say why they are important.

c. Can you predict an important invention in the 21st century?

PROJECT ON THE WEB

Your teacher will give you the correct web-site address. Use the Web and the map on page 109 to find the countries that were part of the British Empire.

a. List the countries that were part of the British Empire.

b. How many countries can you name that use English as an official language?

c. Work in groups. Each group must find out about a different English-speaking country. Show the rest of your class the results of your research.

PLACES YOU CAN VISIT

Here are some places you can visit that are associated
with the life and times of the three monarchs in this book.

HENRY VIII

Deal Castle, Kent: The castle was built in the shape of the Tudor Rose.
Hampton Court Palace, Surrey: It was originally built as a home
for Cardinal Wolsey. It later came into the possession of Henry VIII.
Today many visitors go to Hampton Court,
which is famous for its fascinating maze.
Hever Castle, Kent: The home of the Boleyn family
where Henry VIII courted Anne.
Leeds Castle, Kent: It was originally built as a Norman fortress
and was converted into a Royal Palace by Henry VIII. It is considered
one of the loveliest and most romantic castles in the world!

ELIZABETH I

Hatfield House, Hertfordshire: Young Elizabeth spent
a lot of her time here. Many of her personal belongings are on display.
Tower of London: The Crown Jewels and other interesting collections
are found here. Numerous events in Elizabeth's life took place here.
Stratford-upon-Avon, Warwickshire: Shakespeare's birthplace
and home of the Royal Shakespeare Company.

VICTORIA

Kensington Palace, London: Victoria's birthplace,
where she spent many years of her youth.
Osborne House, Isle of Wight: One of Victoria's favourite homes.
The private apartments are exactly as Victoria left them
when she died in 1901.
Victoria and Albert Museum, London: One of the great museums
planned by Prince Albert.

The Tudors

Mary

Frances Brandon

Lady Jane Grey
1553

Margaret

James V
(Stuart)
of Scotland

Mary *(Stuart)*
Queen of Scots

Henry VII
1485–1509

Arthur

Henry VIII
1509–1547

Edward VI
1547–1553

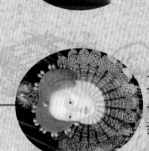

Elizabeth I
1558–1603

Mary I
1553–1558

THE STUARTS

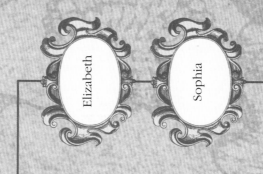

James I
of England and VI of Scotland
1603-1625

Henry

Charles I
1625-1649

Elizabeth

Sophia

Mary

The Hanoverians

James
Edward Stuart

Charles
Edward Stuart

James II
1685-1688

Anne
1702-1714

Mary II
1689-1694

William III
1689-1702

Charles II
1660-1685

Edward
Duke of Kent

George III
1760-1820

George II
1727-1760

George I
1714-1727

Victoria
1837-1901

Edward VII
1901-1910

SAXE
COBURG
GOTHA

William IV
1830-1837

George IV
1820-1830

THE WINDSORS

Elizabeth II
1952–present day

George VI
1936-1952

Edward VIII
1936

George V
1910-1936